Note to you, you wonderful person.
Thank you for buying my book.
♥

Happy Coloring!
~Amanda

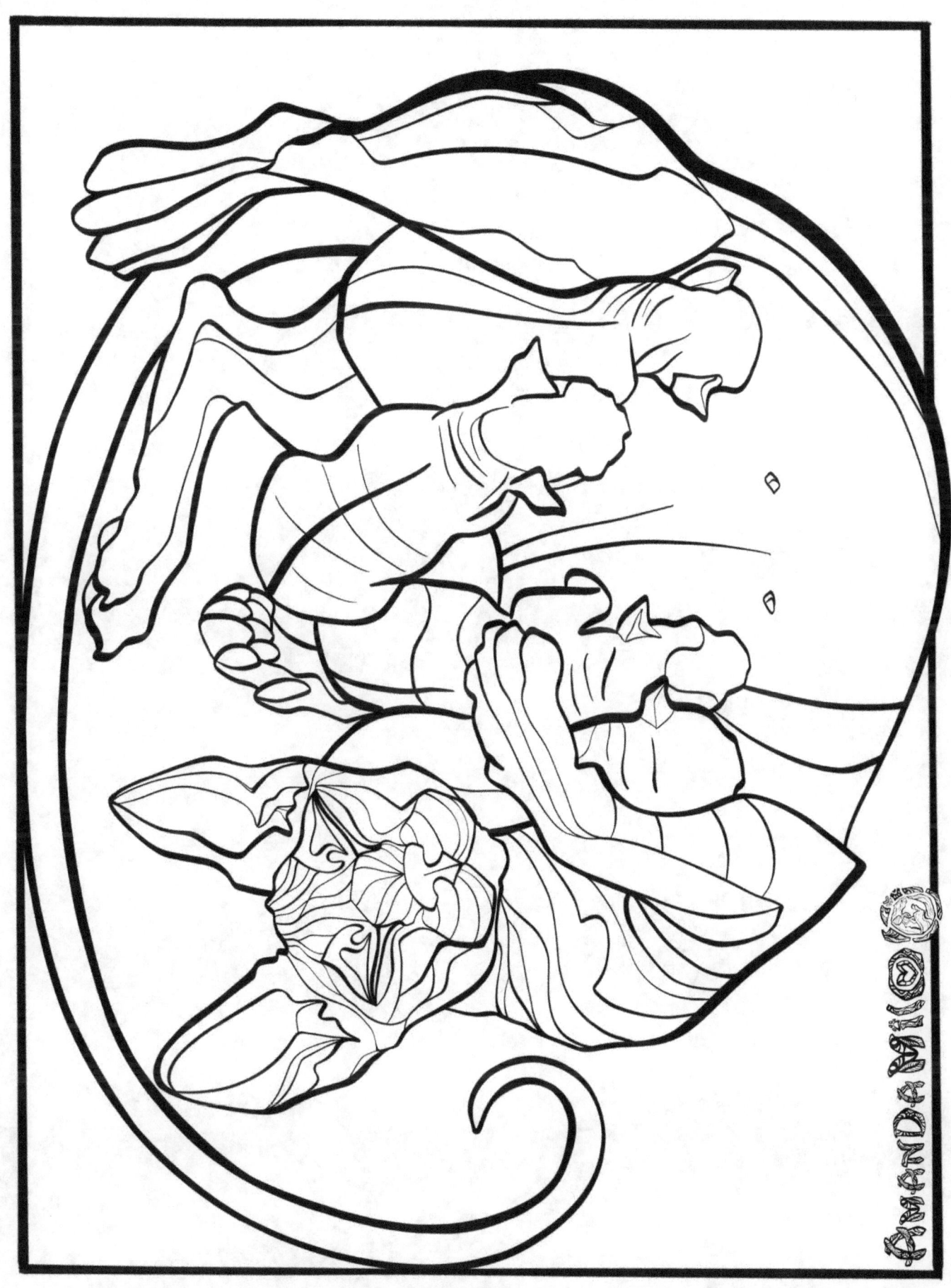

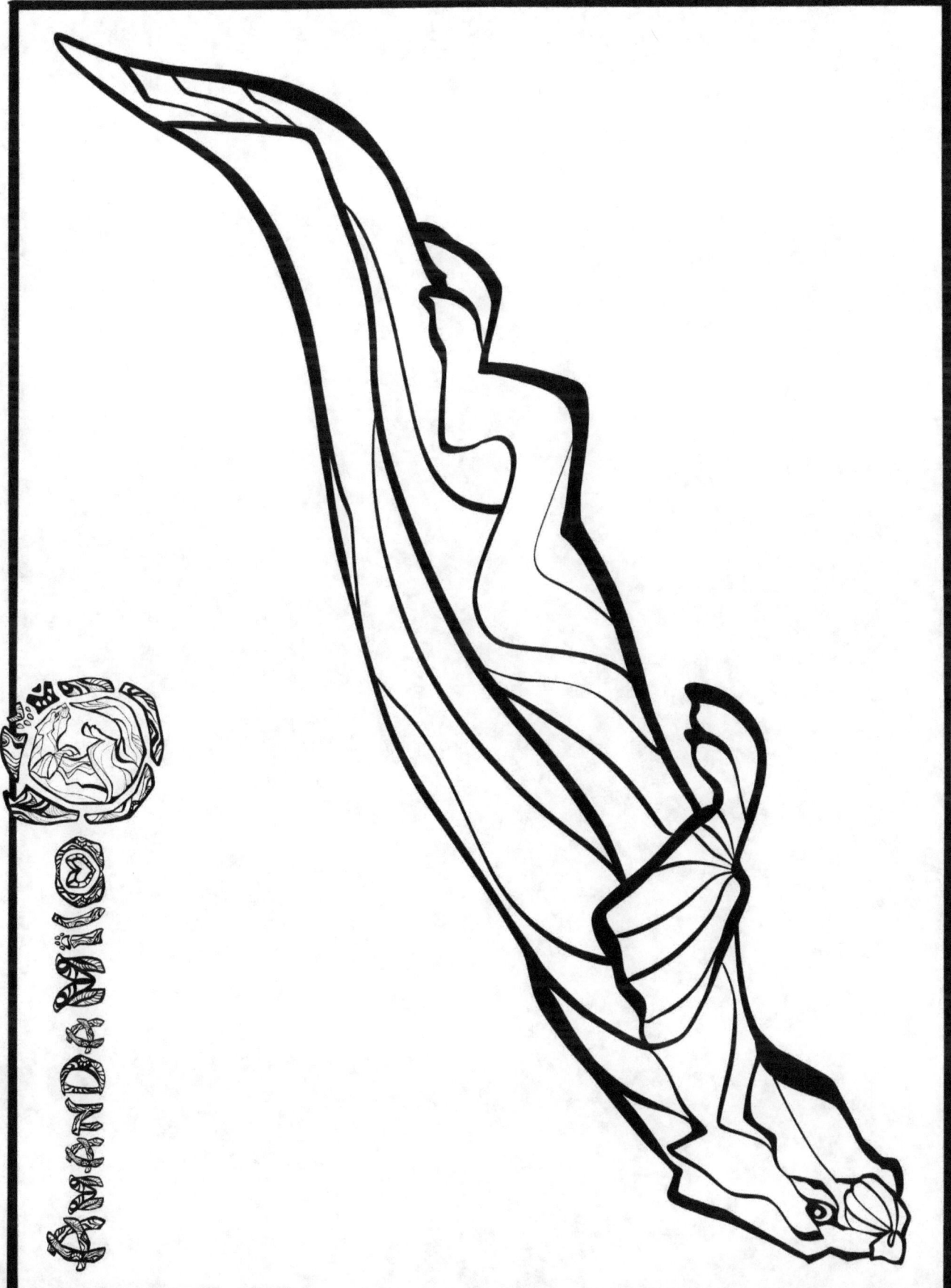

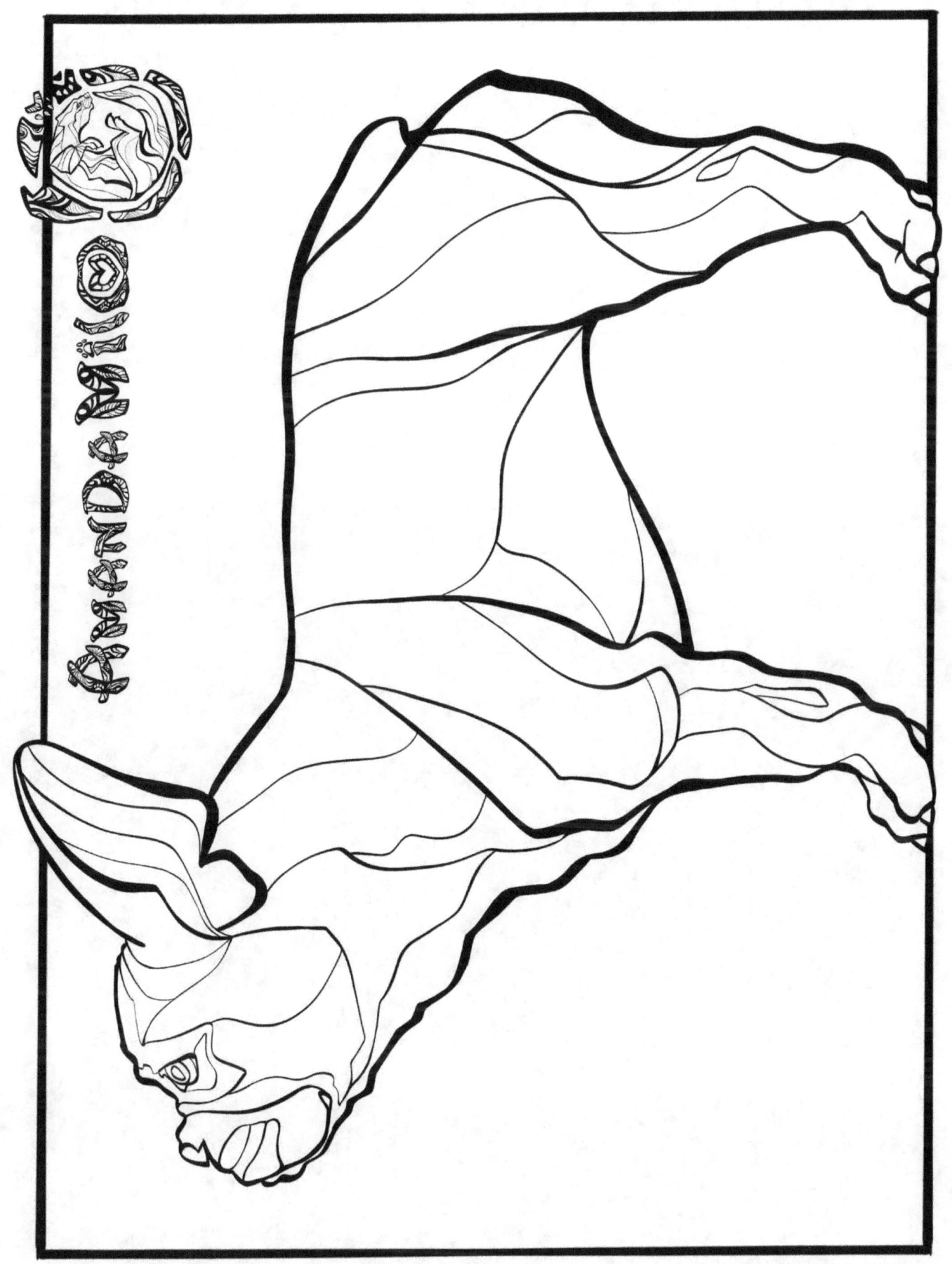

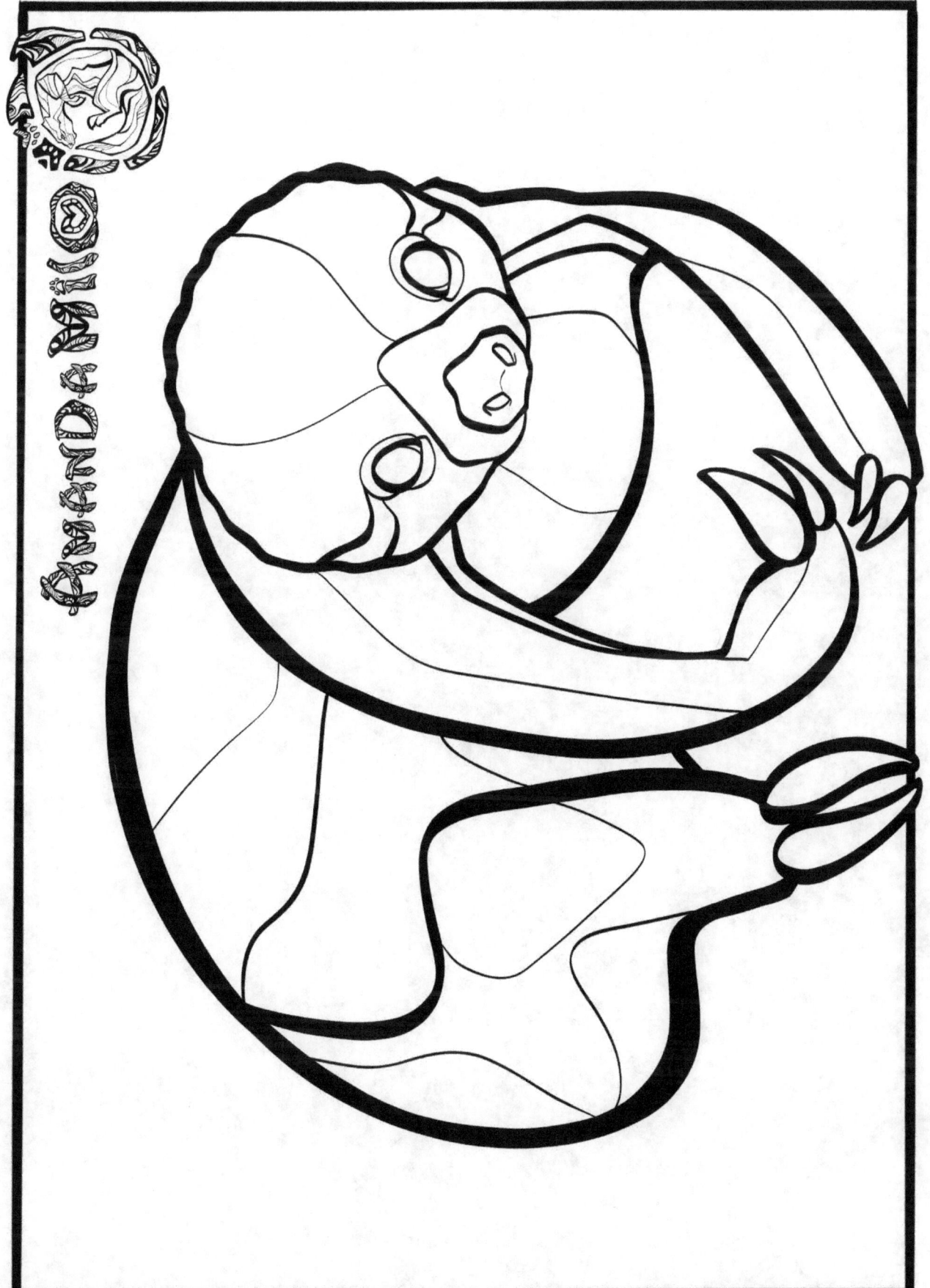

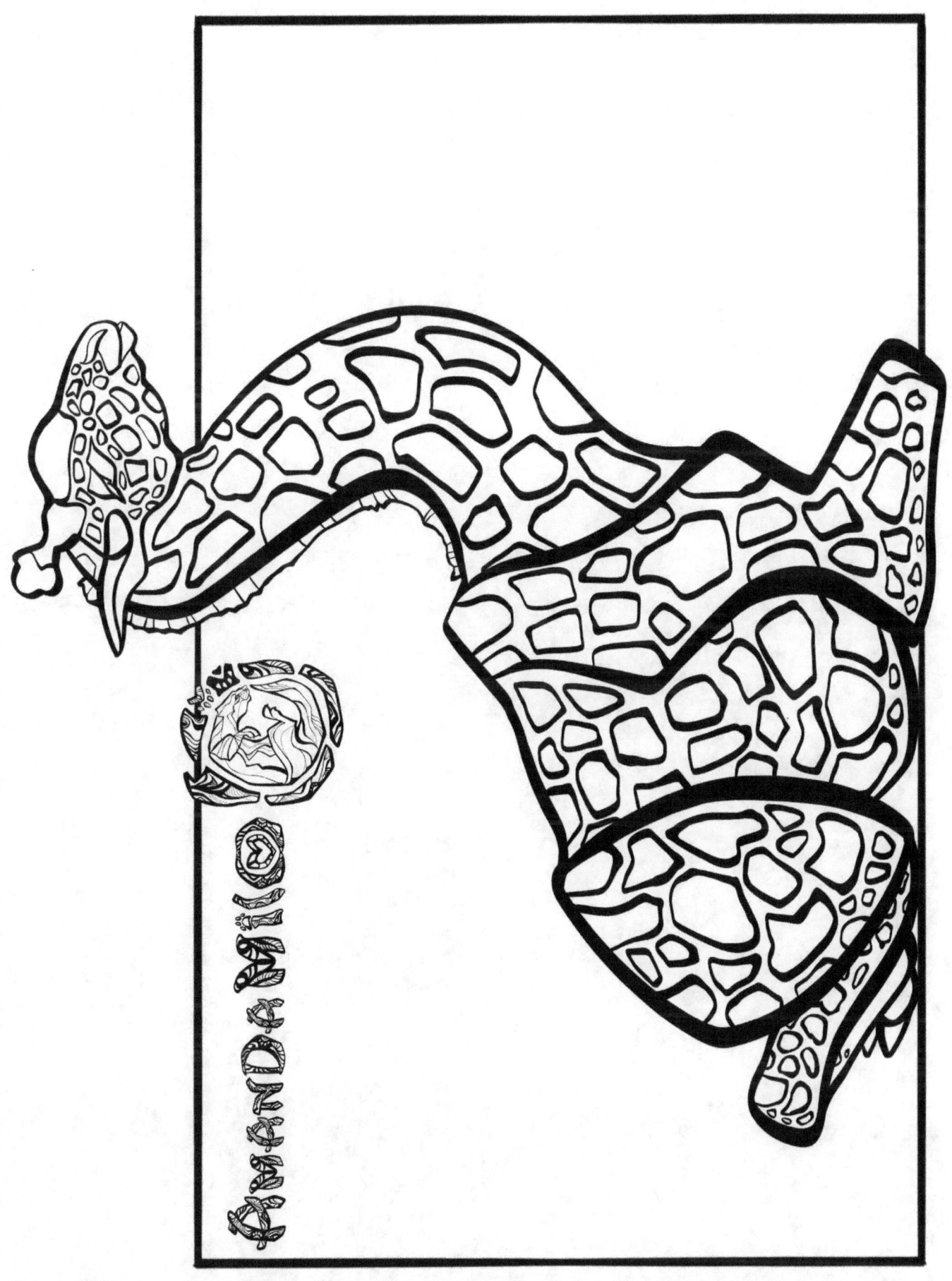

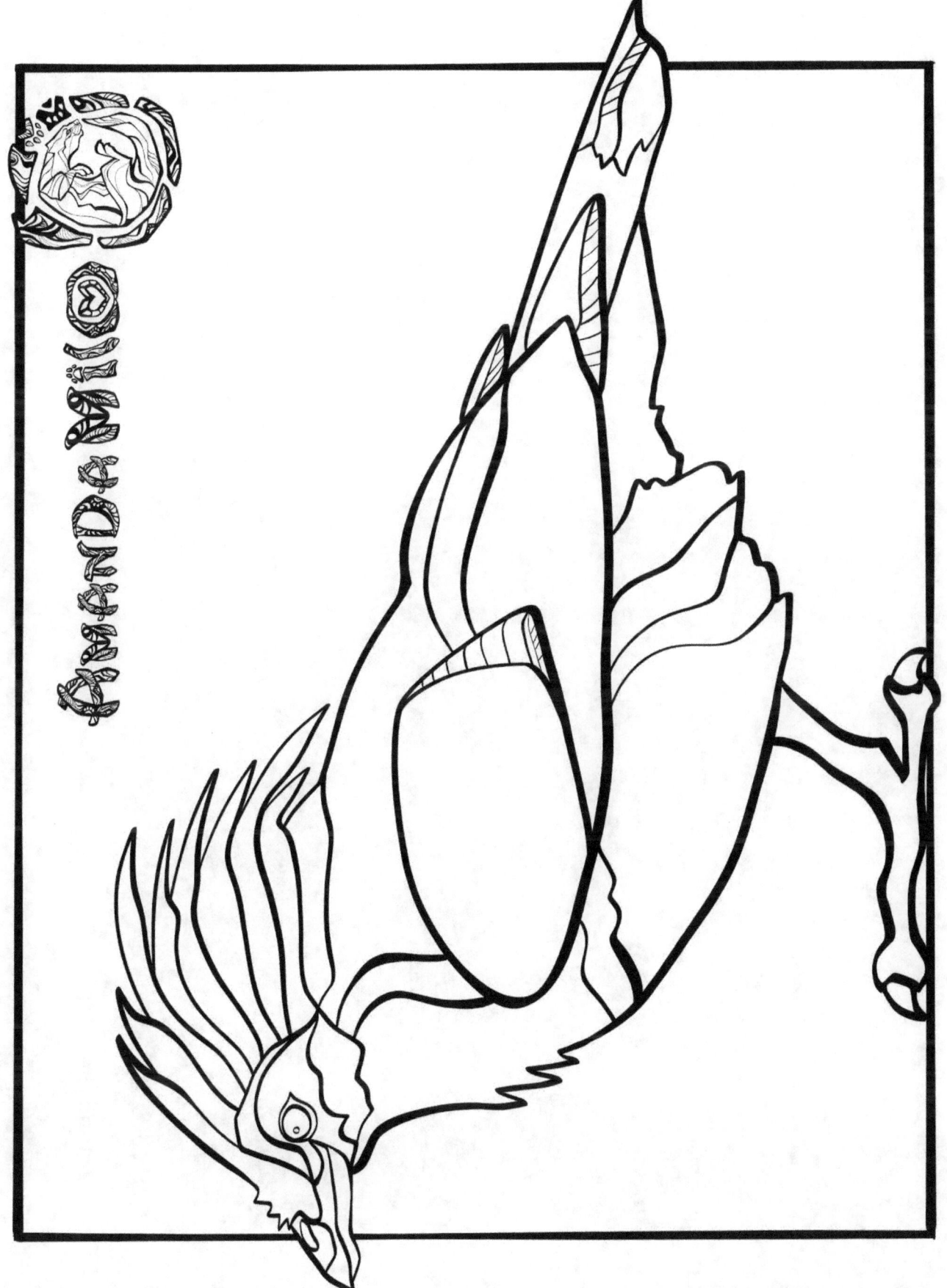

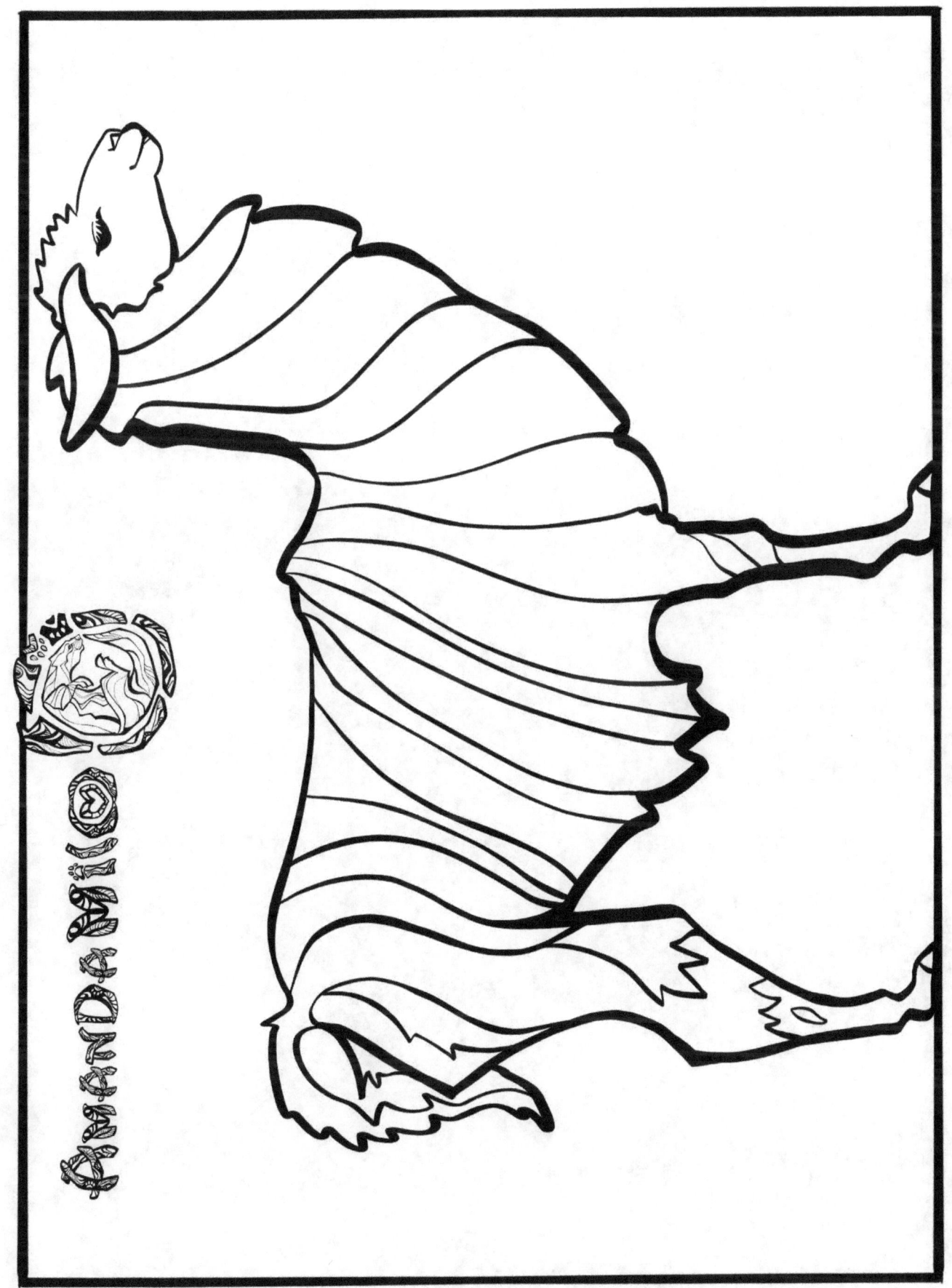

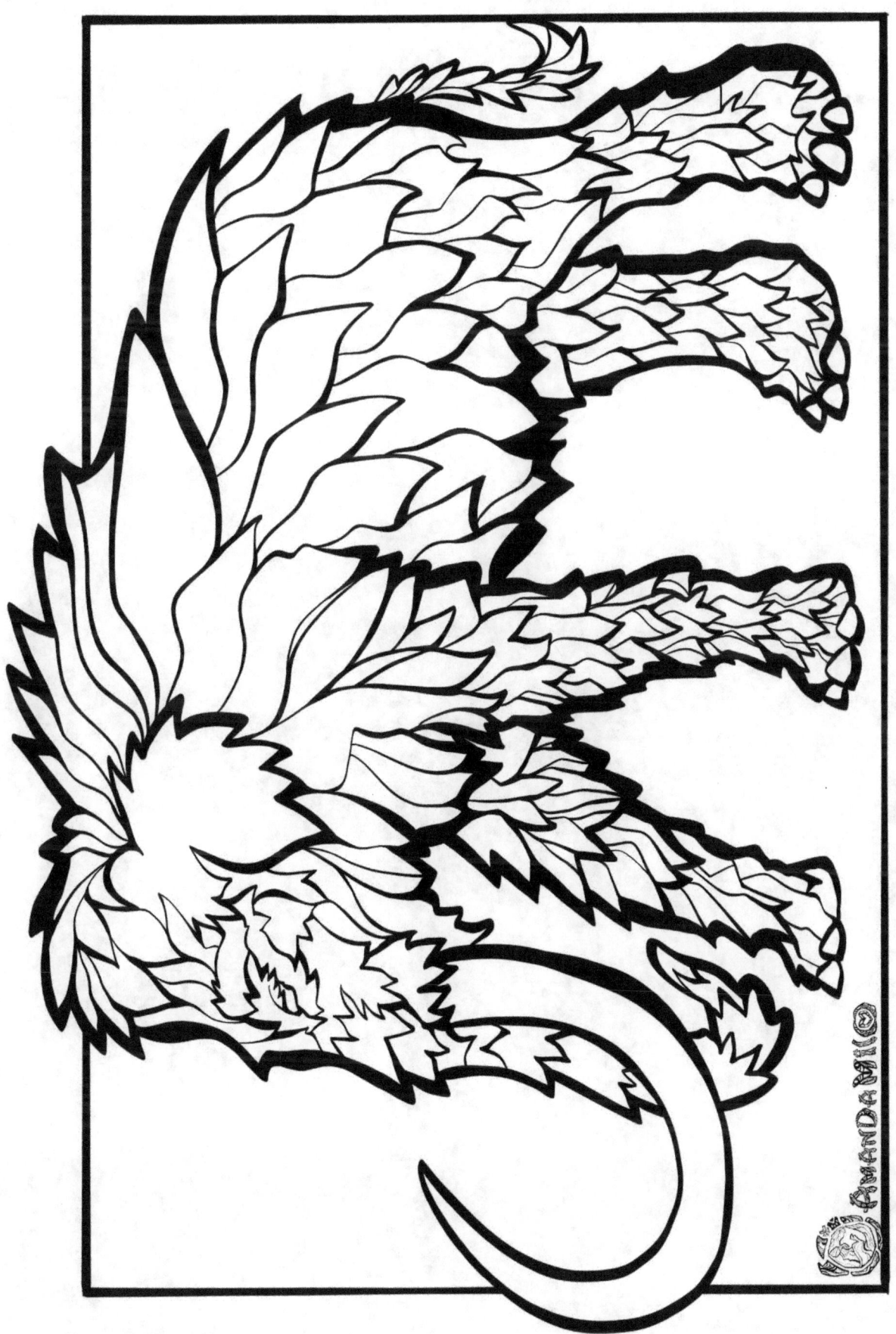

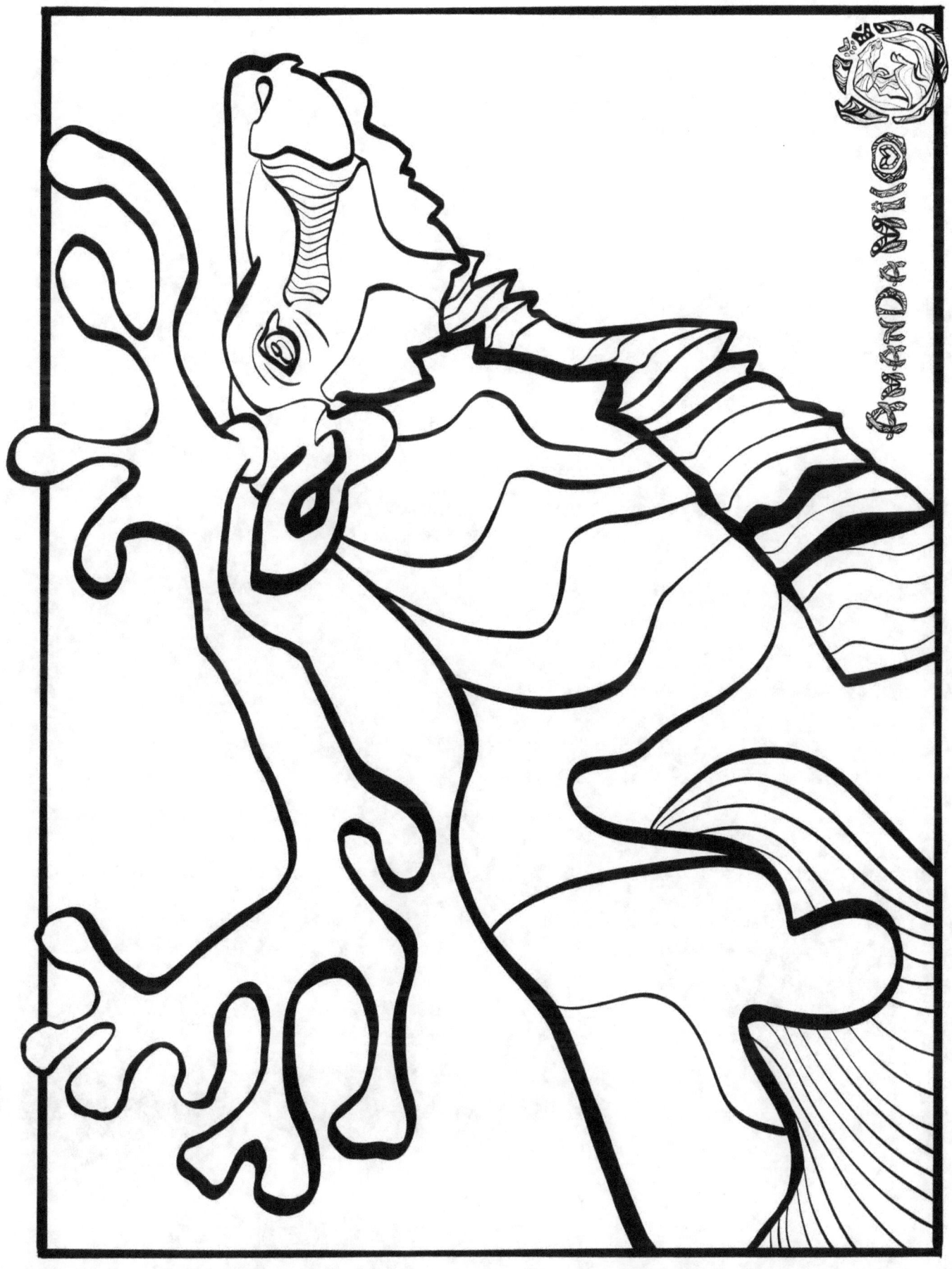

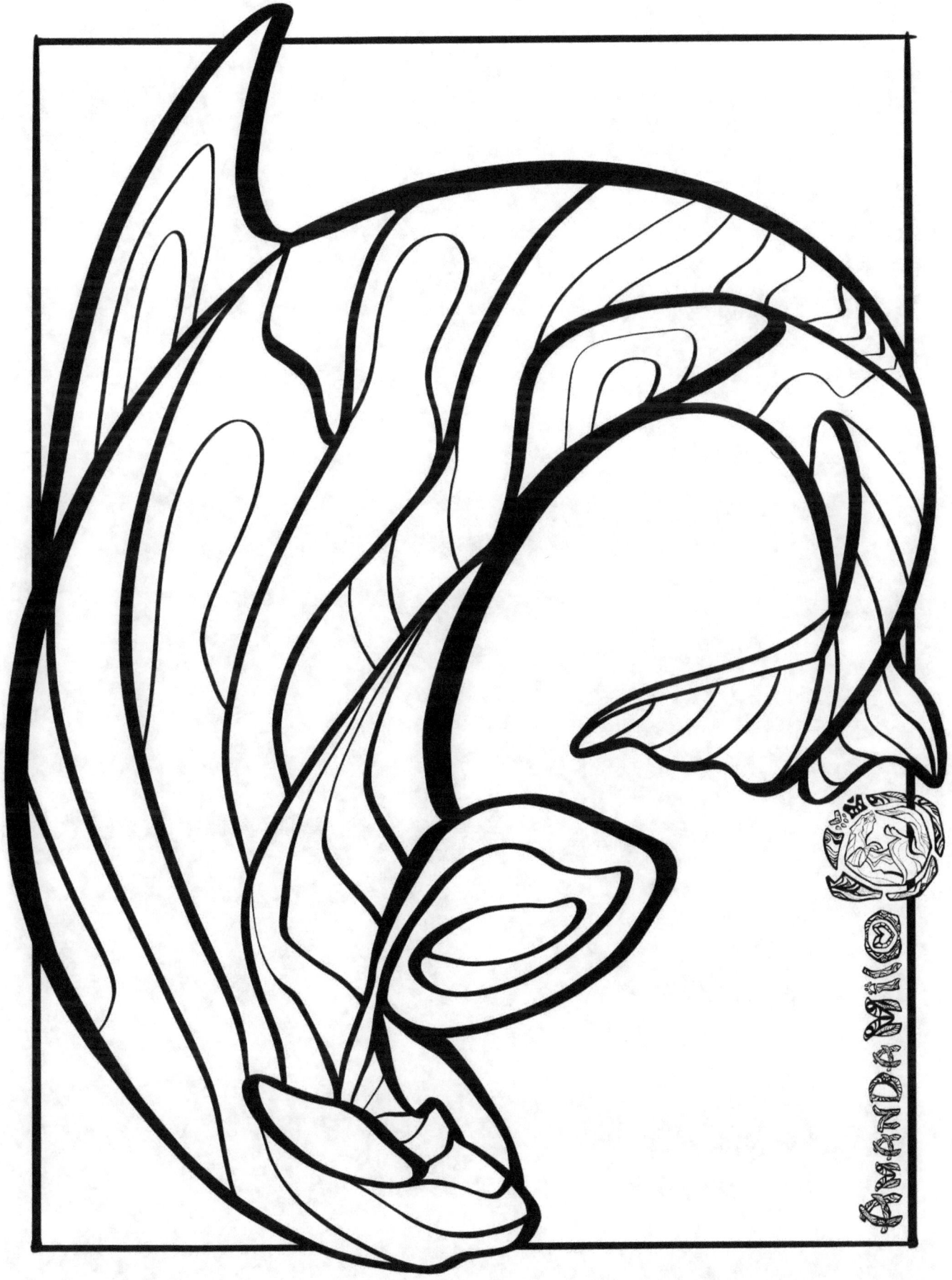

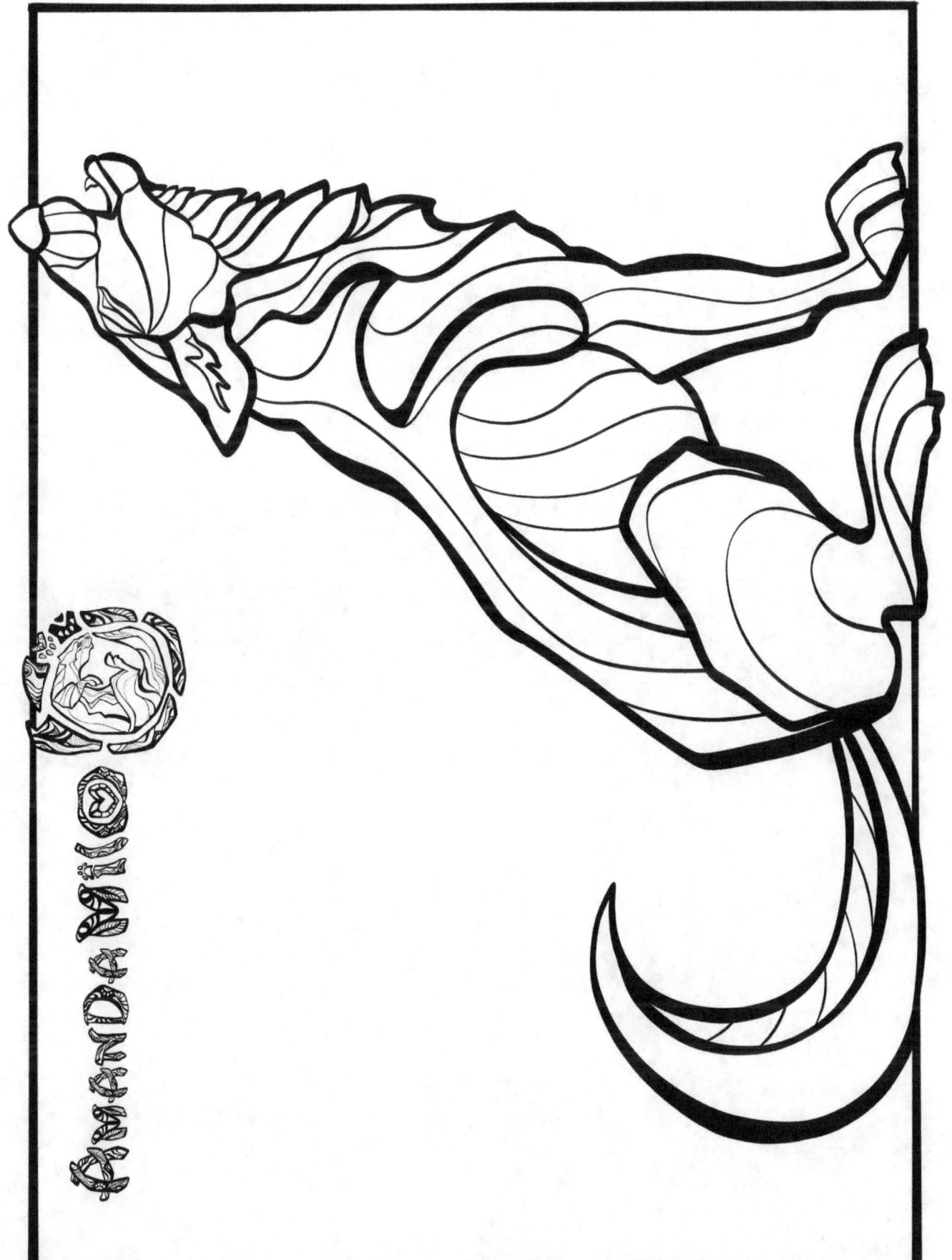

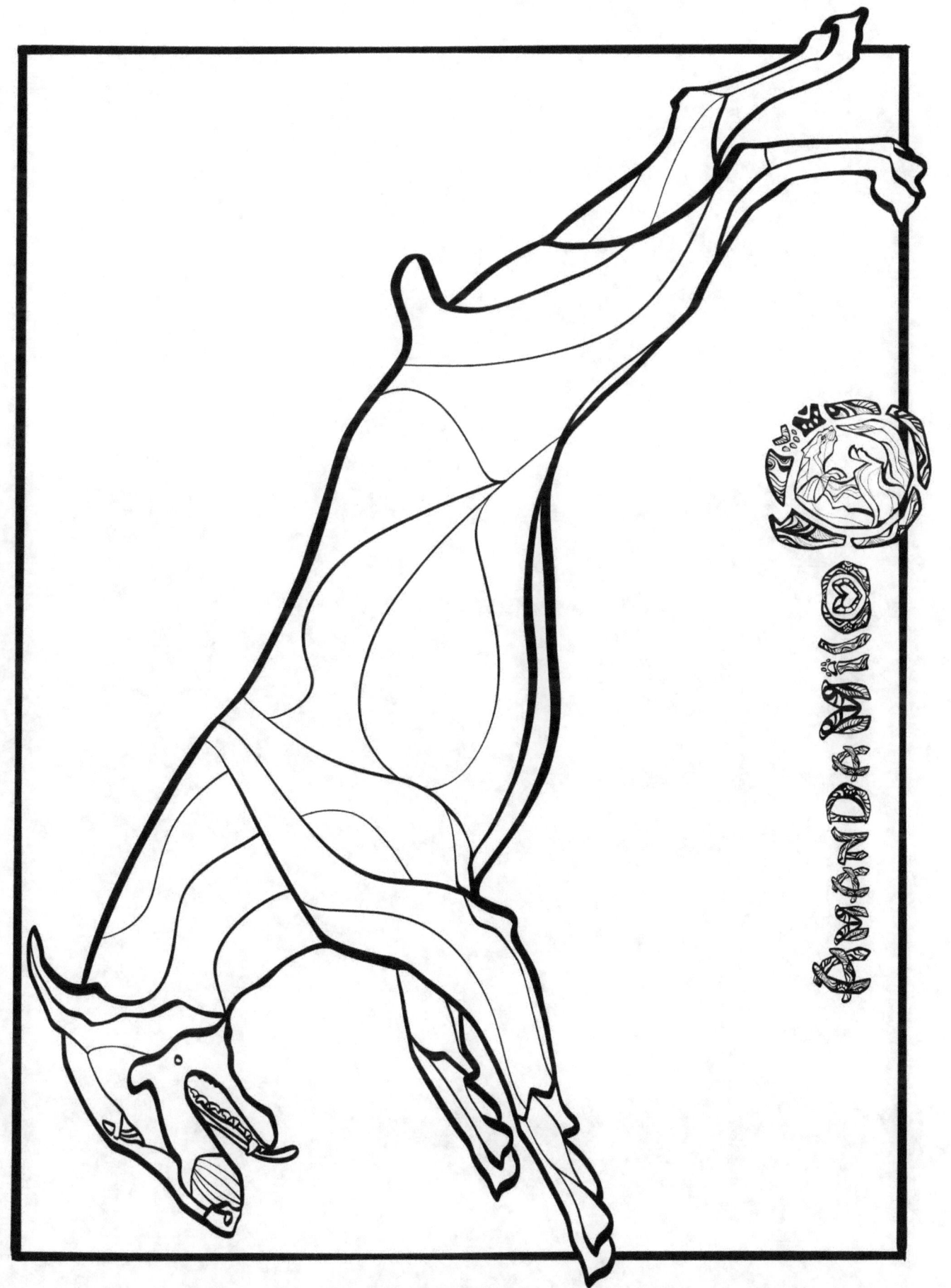

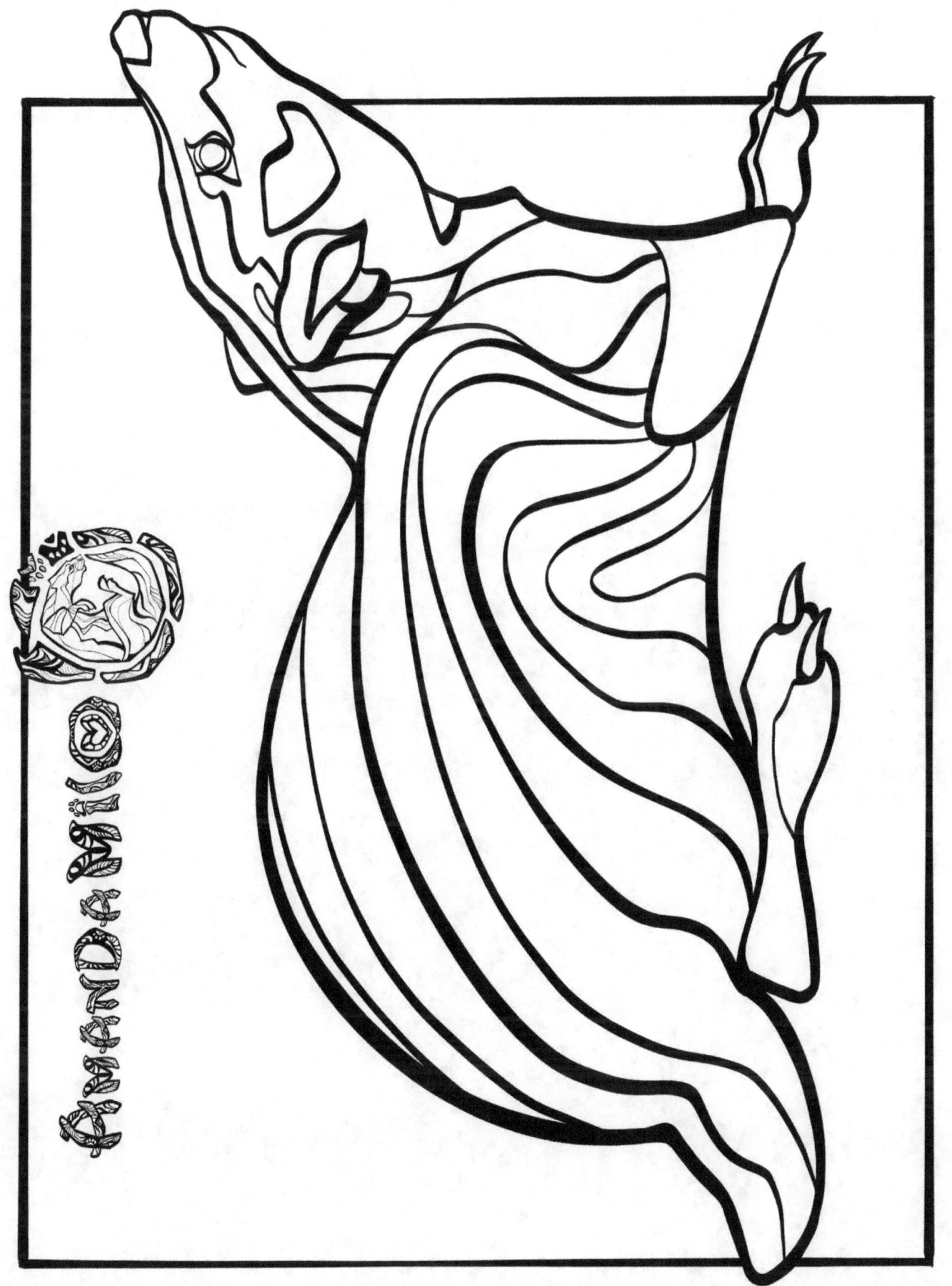

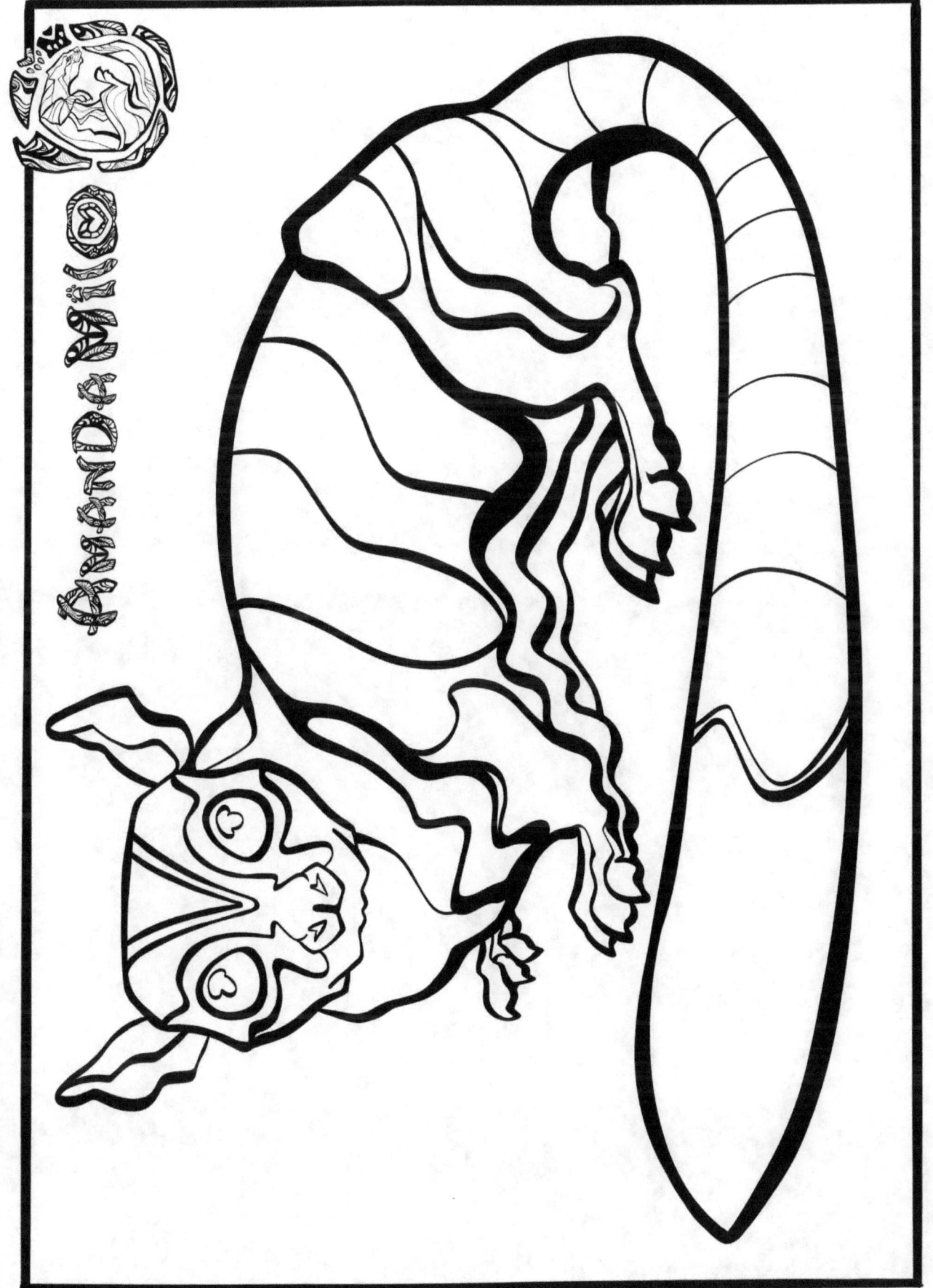

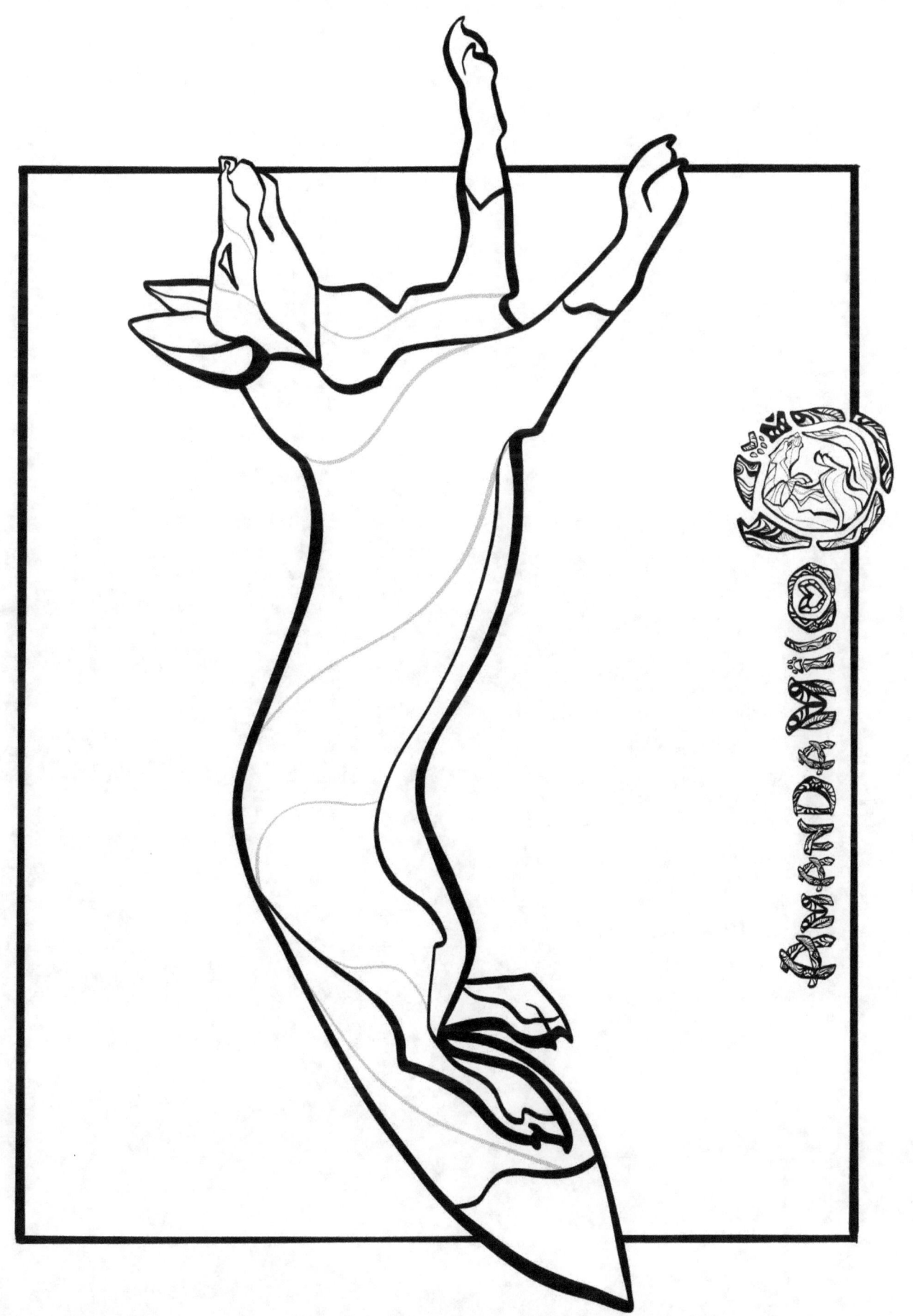

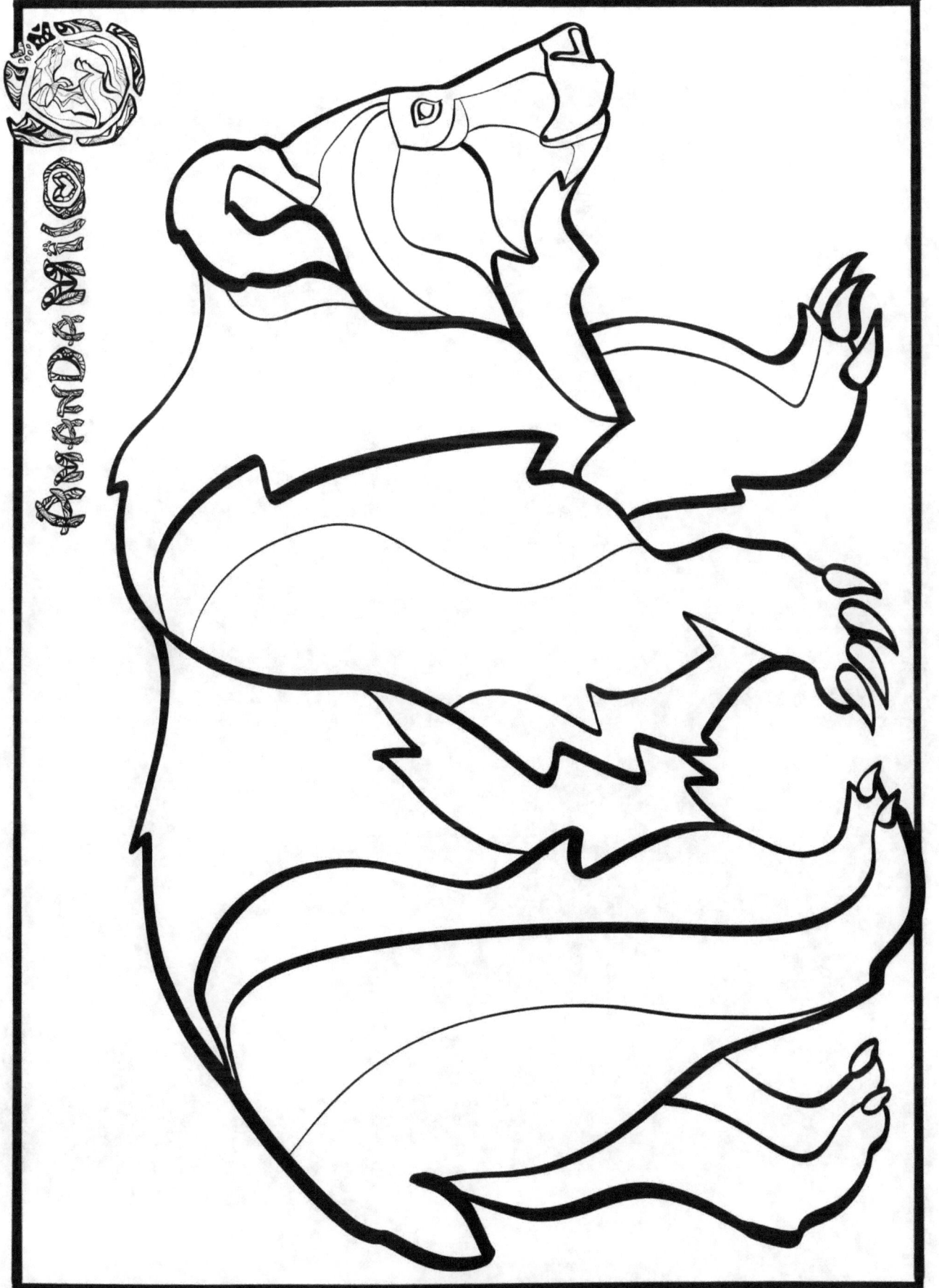

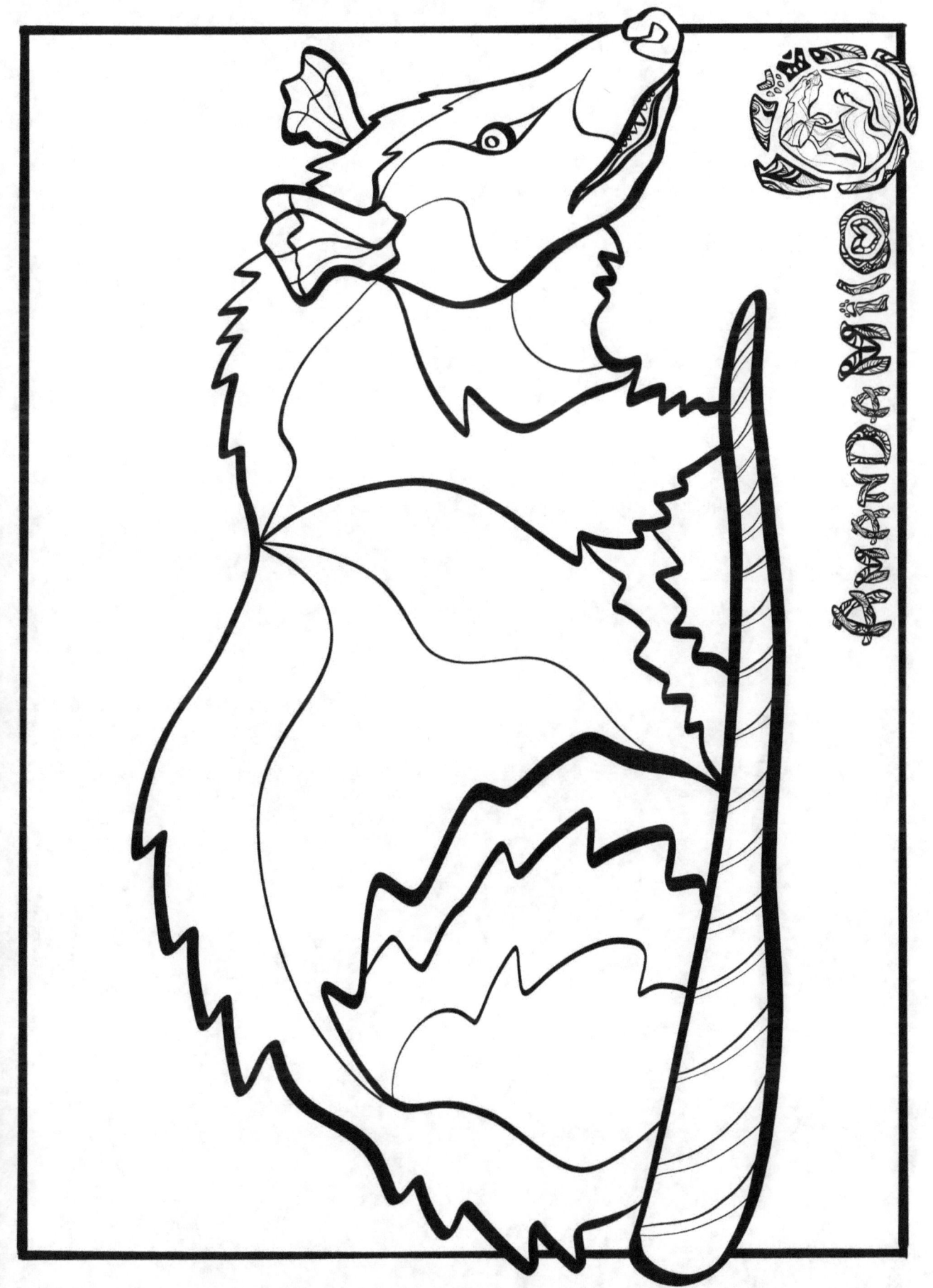

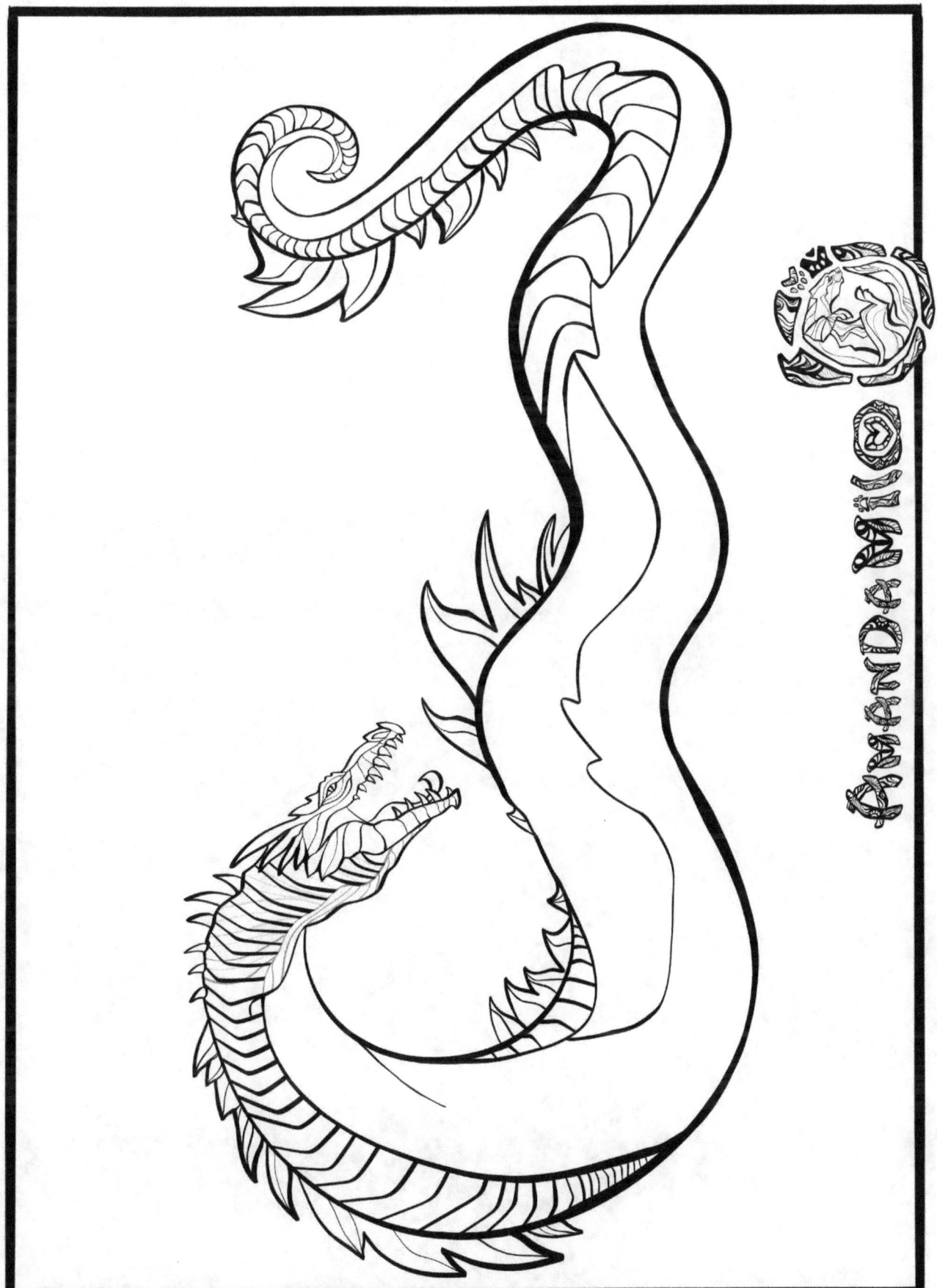

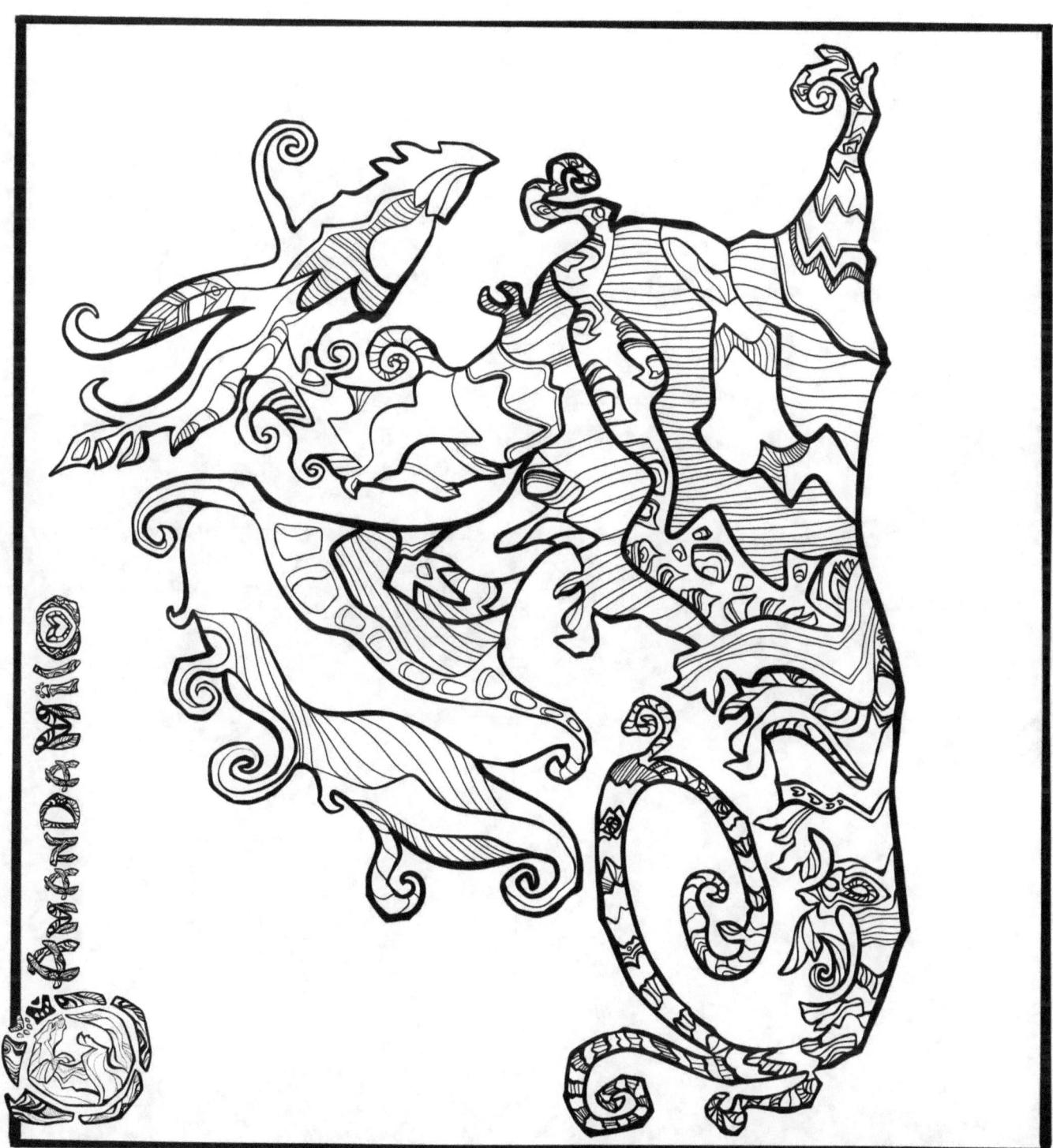

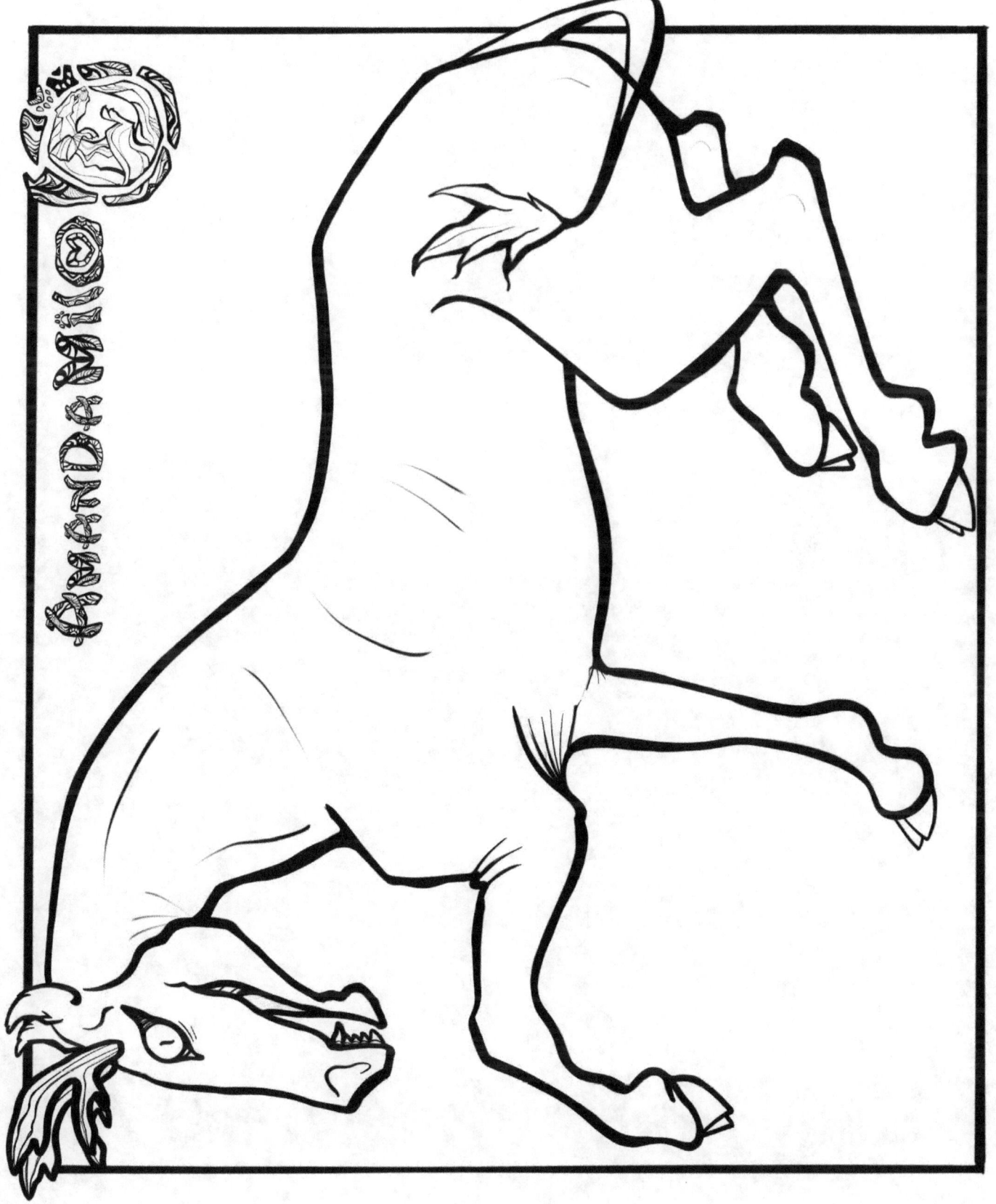

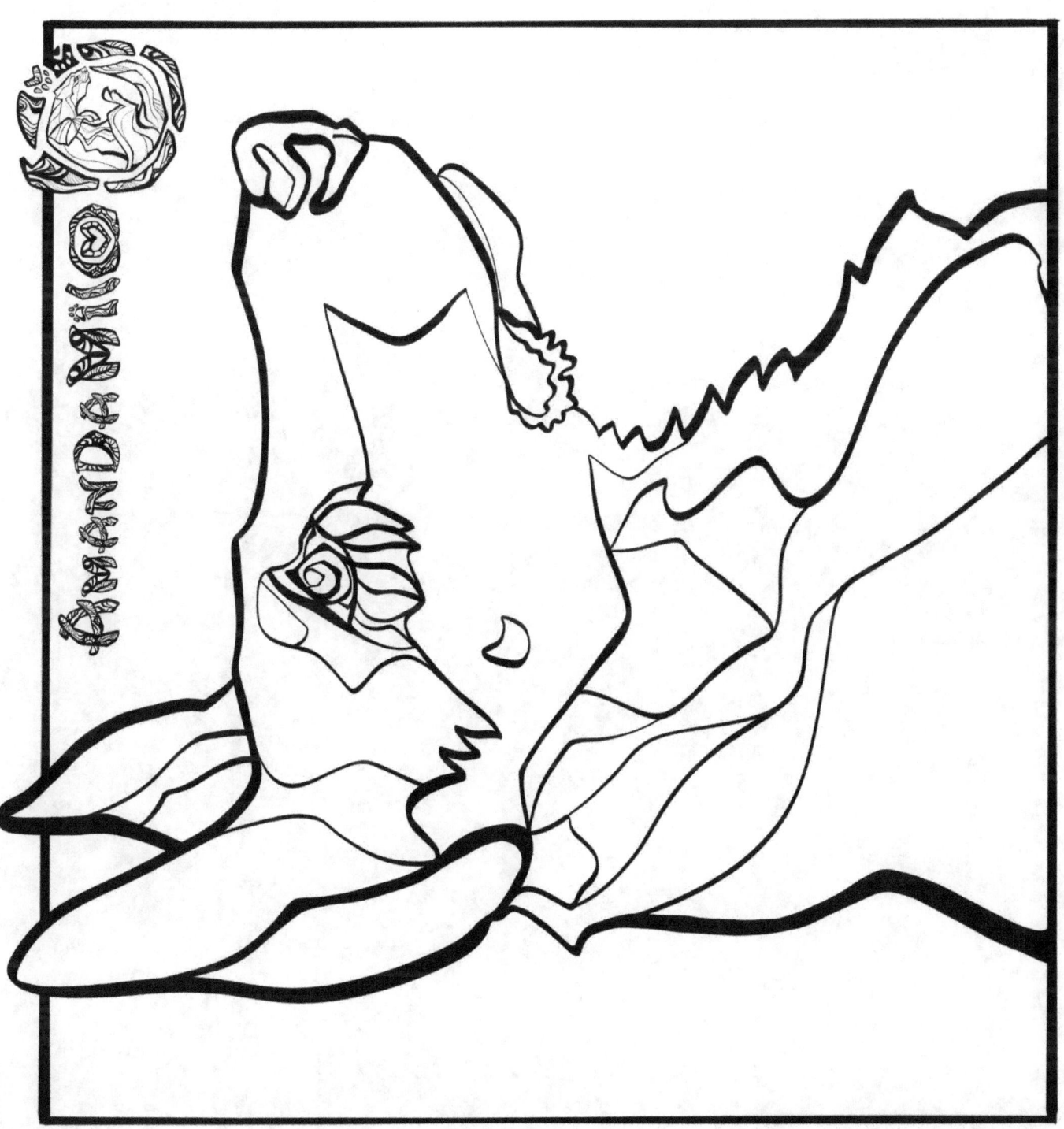

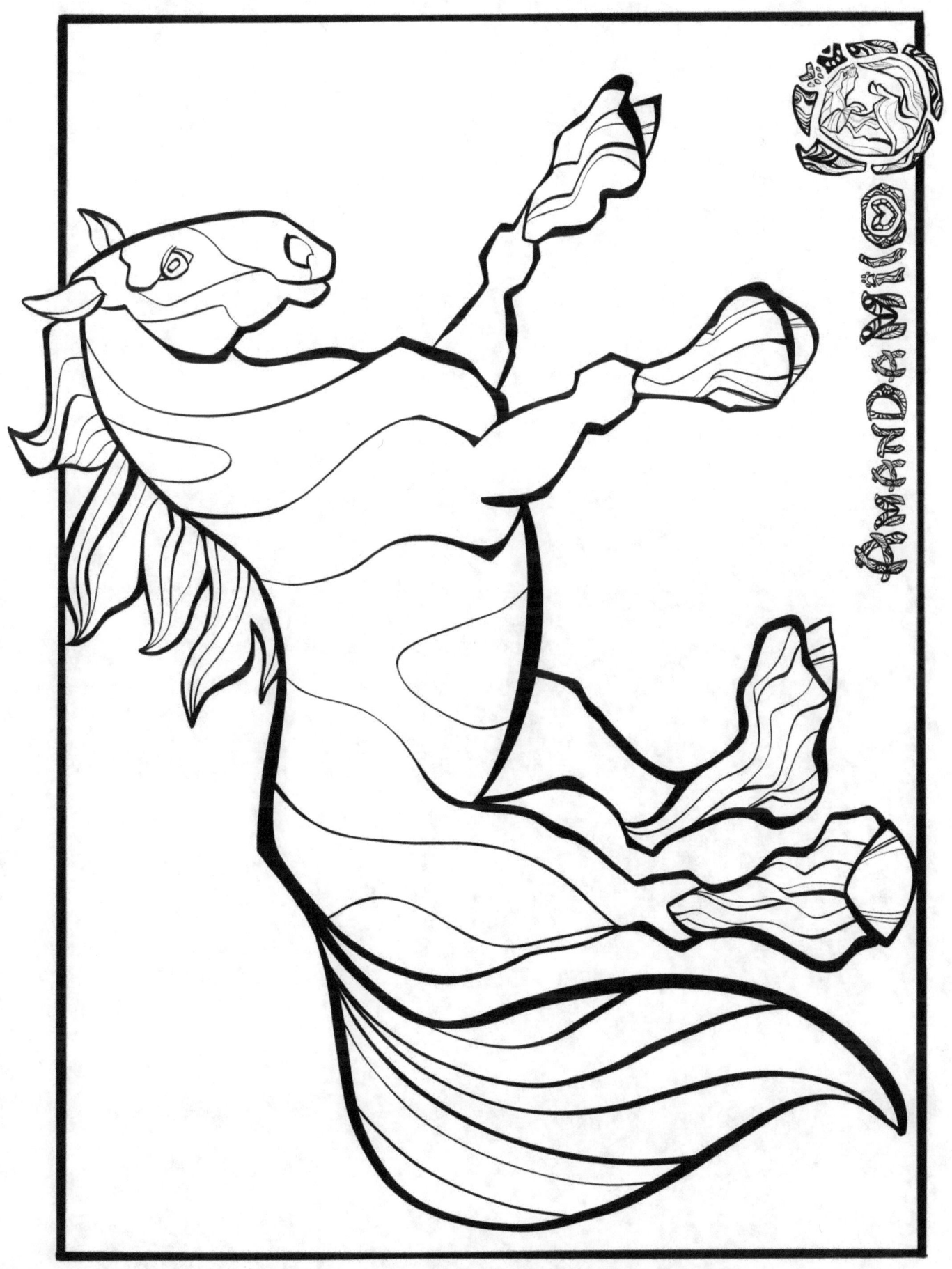

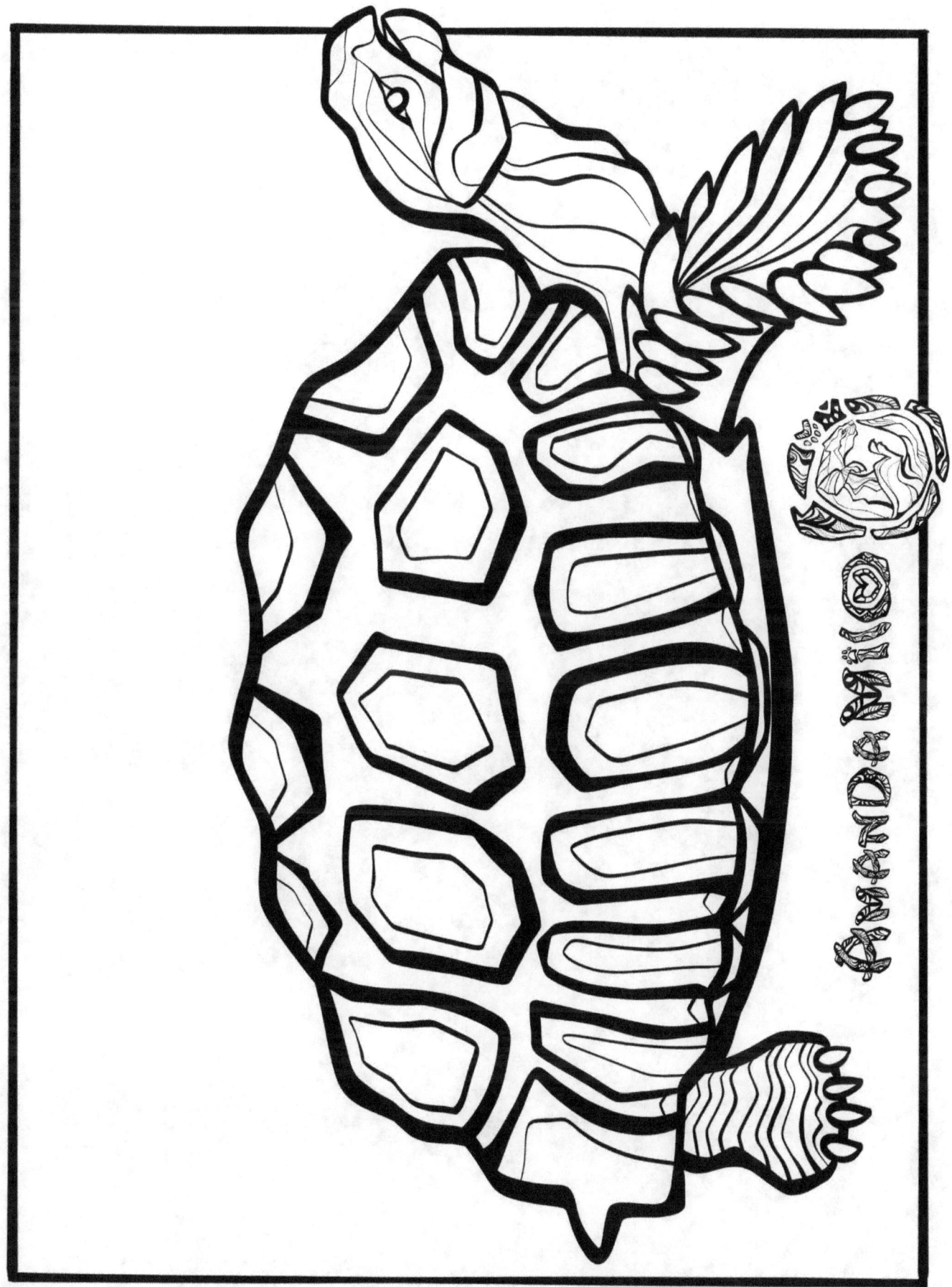

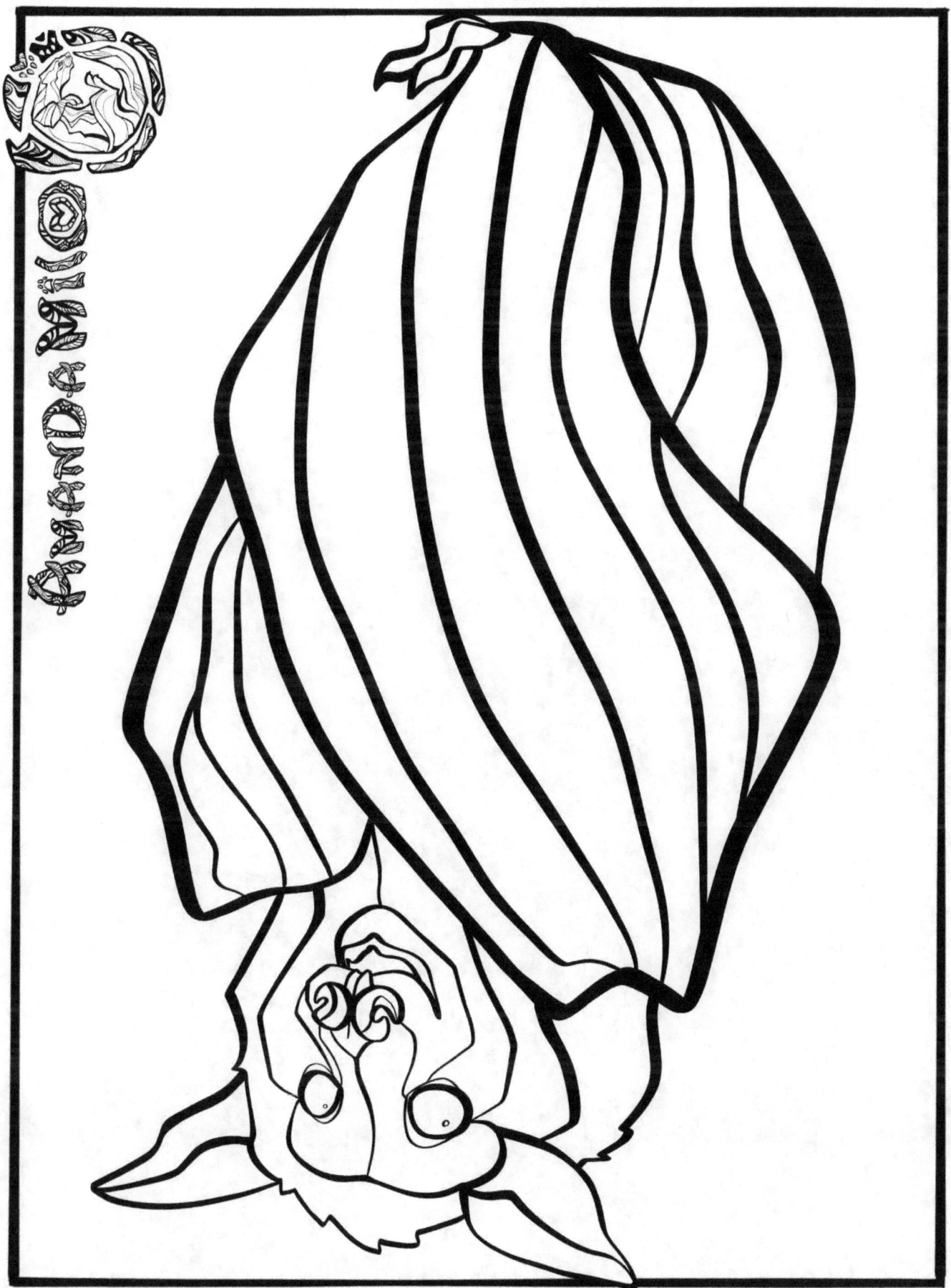

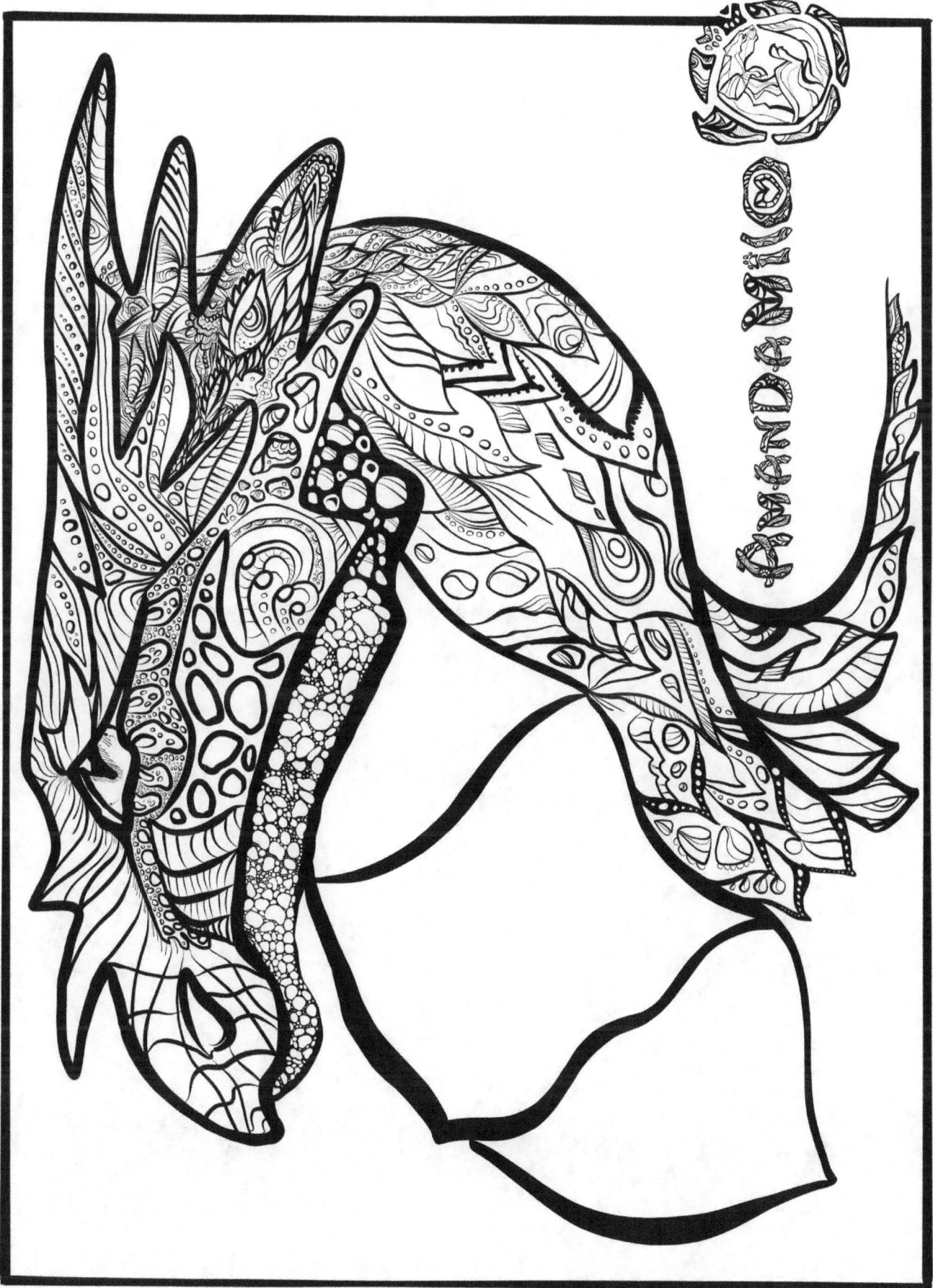

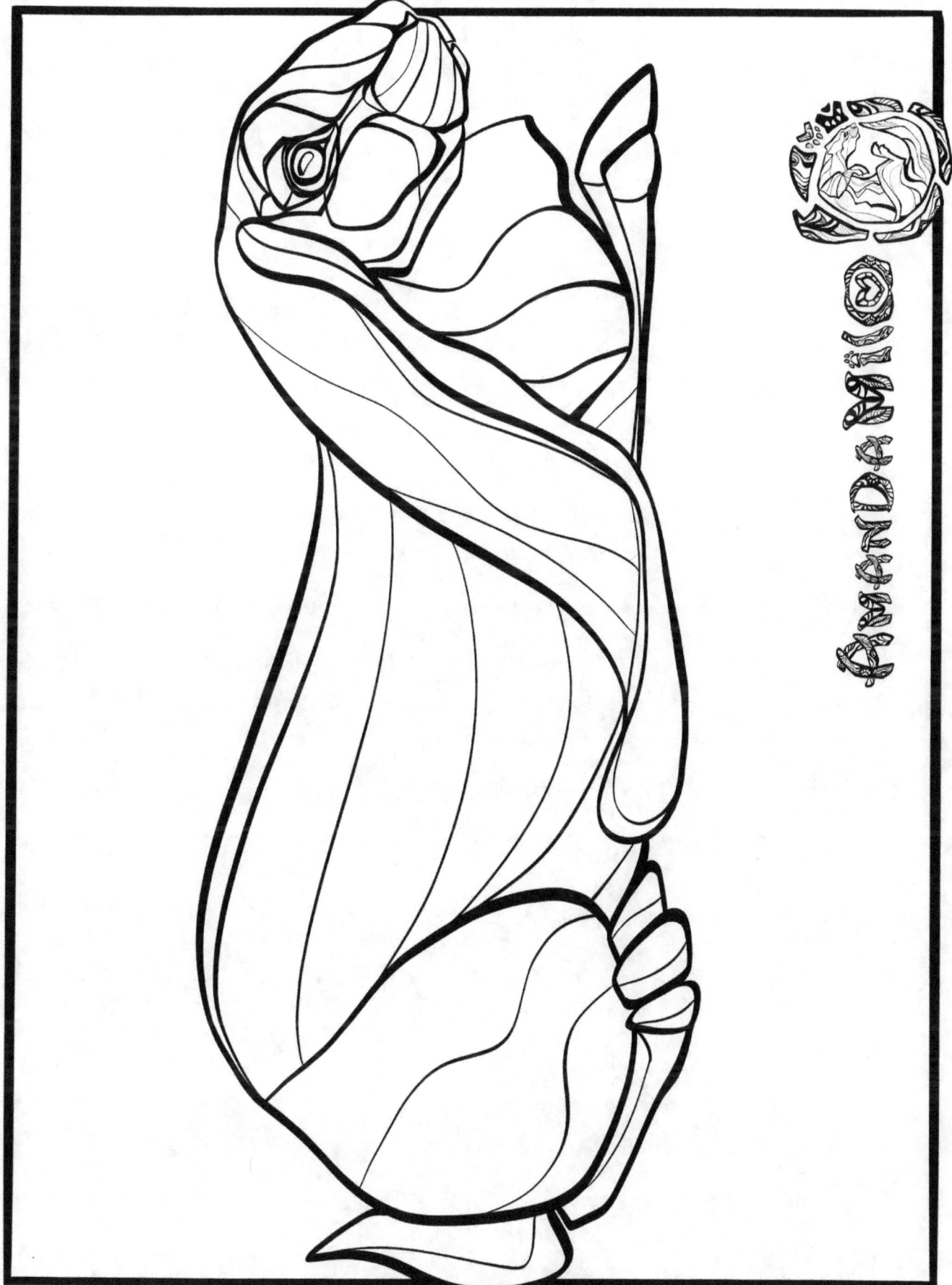

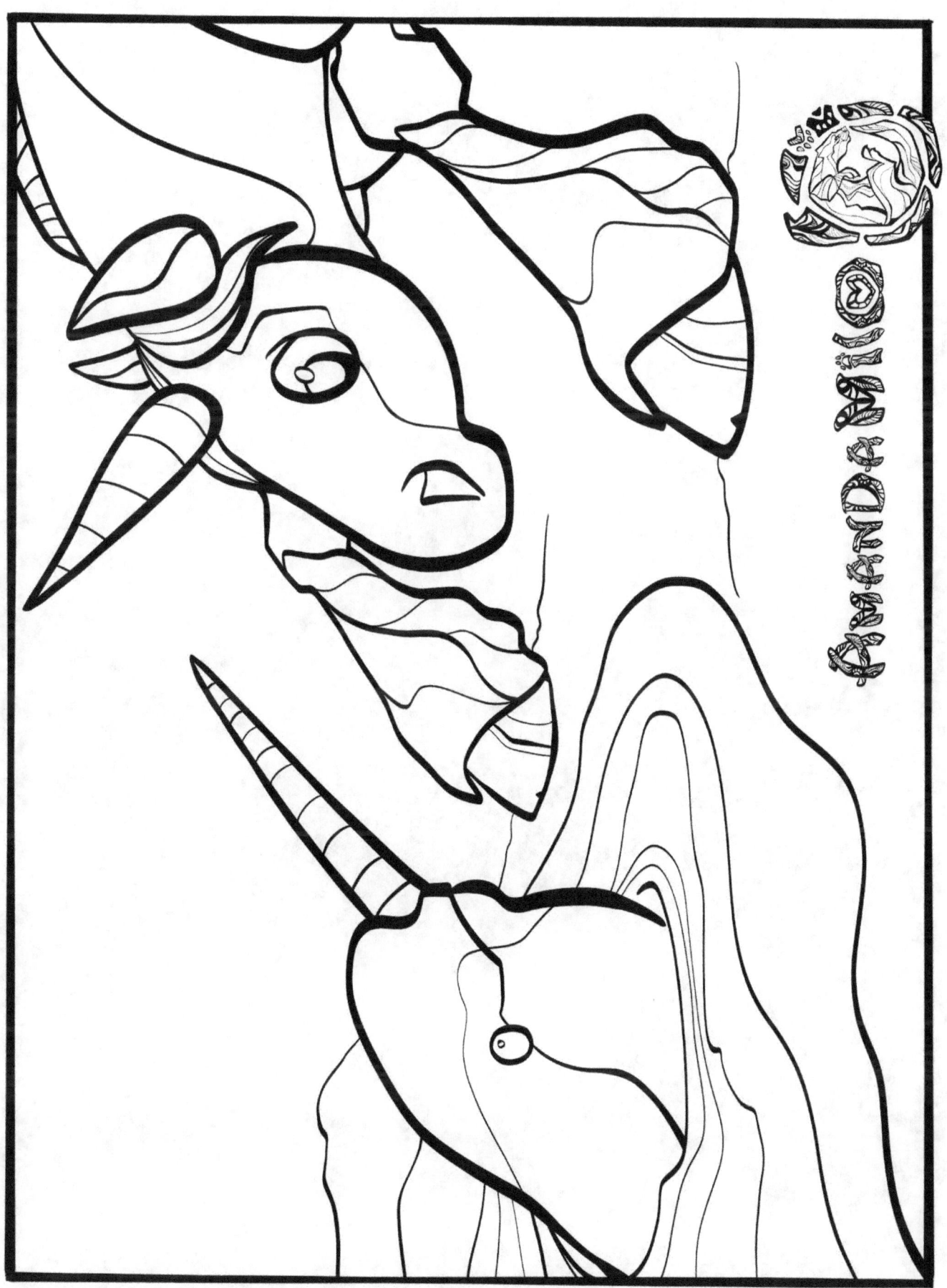

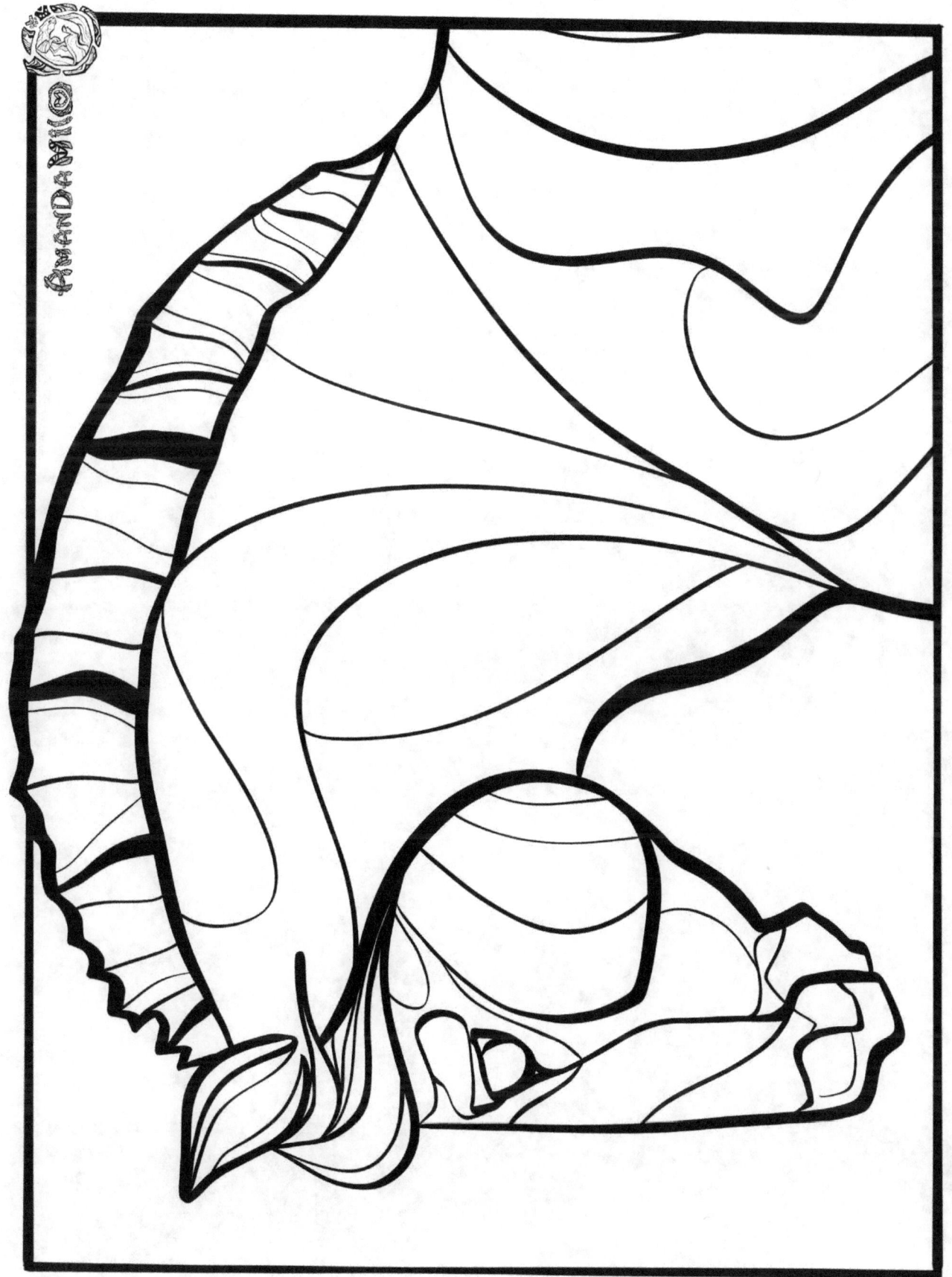

I hope you were able to kick back and relax with these. If you get the chance to leave a review on Amazon, I'd love to hear if you'd like more!
(If you'd like to show off a finished piece, tag me on Facebook;
I want to see! :D)
(I tried to add a link to my FB page, but Amazon said *nuh uh.* XD Sorry!)

Sincerely,
Amanda